~~Adventures in cheap whiskey.~~

Bad ideas and half memories.

Poetry.

By Robert O'Hanlon Jr.

To Joanne,

Thank You So Much.
You are The best,

−R

For my wife Danielle.

To eleven years of strong drinks,

Great sex,

Embarrassing stories,

And always letting me steal your best lines.

Table of Contents

hot the martph e   the

        at first

buhafuc ahhhh"

        I left this in the typer after fifteen beers.
I have no idea what i meant.

        october fifteen, 2011.

Danielle.

My left brain misses you already
Your red underwear
and all the books I was sure you had stolen.

My lady Lazarus [minus red hair]
burning alive, standing there.
Saying no, no, really, I'm fine.
Smiling, smoldering, picking at ash.

You don't talk so brave
when you talk in your sleep.
but we are like children:

Telling the world it only exists
when we choose to look at it!

Or at least we are stunted adults,
emotional retards-
crashing into each other again and again
with vigor- and sometimes; with heat.

At least, we created.

Something. Some devil spawned,

mutant of a love child we called art.

Fucked up

kind of broken

scrawled on a wall

or carved into a page

but still beautiful

in the fatalistic way.

Like rain that falls and threatens a flood

like the murderous potential of bullets in a revolver

like your eyes, soft, after rum drinks

or most terrifying, your voice, meaning *it*, at 3am.

Lips. (homage to Denis Johnson)

Back in the numbed morning my naked lover

tosses her hair and greets the sun with a
middle finger.

Its spiteful Sarah, her voice sweet with
vodka.

Princess of nothing and a terrible tease,

She leads with forbidden lips

As the bottles tip and music rages on;

Like the battle in my skull, over *you.*

And such a night—full of lust and regret.

I wish,

    She were just an erotic hallucination,

Just a fever dream in my broken heart,

Yet she's solid—a mistake in alluring mask.

An exhausting betrayal diluted by passion.

I couldn't expect *you* to understand, forgive.

Just know, when I touch your face, I'm Lying.

Hate Mail #3

Nice shoes.
Its kind of my line
but it seems to work
at least,
on my type.

I attract the emotionally wrecked
Like flypaper made of gold!
I like a dumb girl
Who maintains that she is in fact
Intelligent.

I know sweetie, I know;
Your brilliant.
Now take off your clothes.

Yeah sure, I sound like a fucking prick.
Worthless womanizer who drinks too much
and smokes himself halfway blind.
I wouldn't argue, either
Its all just a ritual in my eyes-

Something to call out the dredges, the rest

Of the fucked up underbelly, who have discovered

We just cant function outside of this for long.

Oh shut up, its not so bad. At least we can spot each

Other; a million miles away, or at least across a bar.

Its the same reasons an entire class used to share weed

right before reading poetry to each other-

Goddamn that professor thought we were all so bright and clever.

If only we could get back to that.

It felt so innocent in the guise of academia

We would all grow up eventually, right?

Ok, maybe not. But we all had good intentions.

Somewhere near the beer, bongs and unclaimed undergarments.

Right over by the forgotten condoms and the shot glasses.

That's it, right there, I swear to God, grab
it! Fuck!

There goes my intention, out the window with
my scholarship.

At least I grew up in America. I'm told other
countries

will kill you or let you starve if your
entirely useless.

So to that I say, God Bless America and pass
the whiskey!

I think I had a point to make here. I used to

fancy myself a martyr, no really.

It was a sad thing to behold. You think I'm
being pretentious now

You should have seen me before I gave up the
Mohawk.

I was full of shit to say back then and I even
listened to myself.

But your shoes, they really are lovely. I'd
sure love

to see them next to my bed some morning.

Ill try my best not to puke on them.

That would just be rude, after all.

Probably worse than whiskey dick and general disrespect.

Your supposed to be a temple, or something, after all-

-right? I think maybe I've done a good thing for you.

Provided a service, as it were.

Maybe I'm the last one night stand with no ambition-

Maybe I'm the last guy with pretty words and drunk blue eyes.

You can go fall in love now, move on, grow up.

There is nothing romantic about poets. Let me tell you.

Anyone who writes love poems is either seeing dollar signs

Or desperately needs to get laid. Desperately, I promise.

Except I wont promise. Not a fucking thing. Not with me.

Who can really say what they are going to do day to day?

What possessed you to do that? Has to be the question

Most commonly presented to me.

I have not been able to answer it yet.

Was it God? Was it the Devil? Was it Plato or Bukowski?

I think it was just some faceless woman,

Who rocked my world and left me crawling in the dark.

Left me as a blind, stunted fucking emotionally retarded child

Destined to never grow up.

Six, Eight, One.

I can feel it all now.
As we lie here.
With the trickle trickle
And the drip drop
You may call us wasted youth
But I think it's just the walls.

The crumbled splendor of this unnamed palace.
Plaster, rot and brick.
You ask if there's rats; furry and mad ones.
But I'm more concerned about the rain.
What are we hiding from, anymore?
Three years have passed since I came home-
To you, with six bullets in my back.

Yet here we are. And here we remain.
Eight inches of water in the cellar
And ever thinning tile above our heads.
Filth, darling; somehow makes us safe.
Why would anyone be here?
Never mind us. Even just to disappear
This is so below us.

Ill pour another drink if you can find
Where we hid the cigarettes.
Why are you still so amazed
That it took three bullets to kill a rat?
He was immense. Ridiculously so.

Nothing moves my heart quite
Like you with a gun. My gun;
You aim so careful. Like Mojito,
Or maybe some femme fatale.
I'm beginning to lose track.

9mm is beautiful on you.
Except in your mouth.
You can't do it anymore, this game.
This hiding and this pain, it's all just
Temporary. 3 years ago it was me.
So fucking temporary. I knew what was coming
And I went anyway. I turned my back to prove
I didn't care. That I wasn't afraid.
It would have been easier, to kill them both.
Than to crawl back to you, and hear you cry

Upon seeing, that I didn't care for the only
one you cared for.

There's such dust on your face but you're
beautiful.

My smoky little ghost and warm-

To the touch. Why we never freeze even though

The roof leaks like you still can't believe.

Was it ever easy, for you

To kiss my neck and say you didn't care?

About what I said, or why I cried

And smashed our only reflective surface

In a fit that still seems far too Hollywood

For where we really are.

Revenge can only be so sweet.

That's why I unload, reload and repeat.

You say I'm not long for this world.

I only say that I loved you all along.

And I am sorry, so fucking sorry.

A Brighter Discontent

I'm not asking for your heart,

Merely the flesh that surrounds it.

If your lips brush mine just right,

I'll fall right into a crush of delusions.

    Gladly,

    For distraction is far better

Than nothing at all.

Sunday with a hangover.

I have no words today.
My muse left with the rising sun,
said:
you cant kiss me like you mean it.
if you keep trying to drown your tongue.

        So I will tell you about her
          b cause in her abscence,
            there isnt much else to type.

  Its just nonsense.
   The parts of me, of anyone who makes the claim
is locked away with that
woman? demon? drug?
w hatever she is, there is only a gnawing
when she is gone.

  a hunger, a pulse; unna tu ral.
overwhelming in its dissent
impossible
to ignore.

                but thats not so much the point
                whats imperative
                whats really pressing
                is the lure.

   how do you make her come back
   how do you let her forgive
   how do you ask her__

        to forget.

 when you know your using her
bleeding her out, page by page, click by clack
if she were here you would have a joke,
something about cannibalism perhaps.

R. O'Hanlon   3/22/11

Let me go.

Put me down,

I don't look sharp

but I am certainly toxic

when mixed with you.

Not one more sip

its already gone too far

Overdose.

Pump me out

scrub me away

tattoo over the scars.

There is nothing sincere about mutilation,

You remember me warm, with fur.

I'm not. I'm covered in scabs,

and I am shedding all my scales.

I am not happy to see you

there are bugs under my skin.

Its sick, sick as shit
that you can just say my name
or show me yours
and I cant breathe.

No longer want to speak

Don't dare eat

Cant even drink.

I just want to puke
I just want to get you all out

Once and for all...

I need [A want ad].

Two Hookers and an Eight-Ball;

For the kind of love we clean up with a mop
and bucket.

-or-

A dirty blonde with a dirtier mind.

(Tall Heels and long legs a plus)

I have:

To see you stripped.

And maybe strangled.

I need:

Something for the pain.

(A pretty hate machine.)

A cure!:

To models and to dreams.

To not remembering the past;

and refusing to see the future.

I want:

War.

Its not violence, its WAR.

I dont:

Want to stop.

I wont:

Ask you to.

I'll never:

Make sense.

Make right.

Make my bed.

I want:

To hit rock bottom;

 headfirst.

And maybe drag you with me.

I need:

Tangled sheets.

Bruises.

And exhaustion.

A headrush.

A syringe.

With hips, lips, violent eyes.

I know:

You know exactly who you are.

Chicken.

Blue, red, pink.

Pink, red, blue.

I always swallow mine

so much faster than you.

Hey look: two at once.

I'm good at this game

Suicide it would read

if my obituary came.

Now a green and a red

and a white one too.

I'm not a doctor

How should I know what it will do?

Just tilt your head

and down the hatch.

Here comes my girl,

with a fresh little batch.

Now we have purple

I see bad things in the future
no turning back now
We are locked into misadventure.

Hold up, if your sick already;
then its now to late.
Panic should engage,
Where the fuck is your date?

Pills don't work like pot.
They have half-life, Time release.
But they go down just like candy
Thanks to that hard coating of grease.

Oh wait that's right,
There's nobody home,
Is it really chicken then,
If you play it alone?

And that girl with the plate?
What of her? Has she gone too?
Nah, forget her.
She's just a ghost, some ex-lover.

I couldn't write her name

even to say its her fault.

I just want her out: of my prison:

of my head, my heart, my vault.

Vault? Now whats that?

The safe place, the one for my muse.

She got in there once, tainted the whole place-

rubbed herself on everything, left it lit like a fuse.

I've tried to drown her out

smoke just drives her deeper.

Crystals excite her-

but pills can deceive her.

I just want her out.

Does it have to be this hard?

Just what was God on,

When he dealt me this card:

Obsessive, maybe compulsive;

Add blind to the world.
Red flags look like fireworks
When he chooses his girls.

Thanks a lot, you fuck!
I guess feelings are mutual.
Fuck you, fuck me-
I yell at God; does that make me spiritual?

Thorazine is a joke,
Haldol is for pussies.
My brain is made of cement
not something pliable or mushy.

Your not listening Doctor!
Oh fuck, I smashed a mirror.
Still here, just me.
Shit, look at that sliver.

I wonder about my blood
all stuffed full of prescriptions like a pie.
If some sick fuck drank it,
Would it get them really high?

I'd feed it to Her.

Shes there, on the edge of my vision.

Maybe I can catch her,

Then drown her in the kitchen.

Drive Home

We kiss through heavy smoke,

Goodbye to lethargic comfort

And timeless sense of nothing;

Nothing- what I leave you for.

Wheels grind through damp streets,

Two lane blacktop bathed in yellow glow.

I choose the middle, an erratic folly?

Yes. Death wish? Perhaps. Mistake? Surely.

Miles and miles and miles to go;

I don't care where, just far.

Home faded into the fog at fourteen.

I'm just sick, missing a place that doesn't

exist.

Digital green mockery needs to know;

Why pussycat, is there no satisfaction?

What is this misery I miss so completely?

That hurts like hell but melts in my mouth.

Where is my saucy bruised little belle?

The girl with tired eyes and smoky fingers,

The one who always gets me off when I'm down.

Perhaps she died, at age three, rather than

meet me.

Home as always, silent and alone.

Even the cat fails to stir as I stumble in.

Where is my warm welcome? Where is my warmer

lover?

It's gone away with age, and she's just a

ghost on frosty sheets.

So what is home? Other than anemic

distraction.

It's a roof of static, a floor of angst,

Walls of noise and windows of sudden panic.

There is no smiling mother in my kitchen.

Perhaps I shouldn't have survived the ride,

Ungrateful as I am for these walls and roof.

Maybe a foot to the left into oncoming light

Would have been a fitting, unfeeling

conclusion.

But what then? Heaven is not my home.

And Hell is just a day's drive from where I

lay.

So I survive, I return to whence I came

For tomorrow is always closer than yesterday,

And maybe home is just another mile away.

S.D. Art.

I've found myself a new Devil.
One with ruby toes
and a spine like a zipper.

-But not a healthy zipper. Certainly not new.
Not one that functions or opens
to something worth hiding away.
This is a broken zipper,
with a snag that hooks and tears skin
and exists only to leave things raw.

If you breathe her name
She will try to choke you.
That's only fun, like, twice...

So you don't say her name, never.
Shes not the kind of Devil you call
into existence with a spell or a poem anyway
Oh no, oh no.
She finds you.
Comes slithering into your bed

when you are exactly too fucked up to care.

That's how she really gets inside
One sweaty bite of your soul at a time.
Until there might be nothing left.

Breakdowns can be so beautiful.
That slow motion spin of your entire life
like the panicked moment when you realize
you have lost control and cant get it back.
Your spinning and coming apart at the seams.
And shes right there:

With a hand on your shoulder
With a foot in your crotch
With a lip on your ear

Pushing you faster, ripping your hands from
the wheel
Cutting the brakes and screaming with laughter
when;
Finally,
It all has to come to some catastrophic and
screeching halt.
Annihilation, in a pure and cathartic sense.

She will call it a rebirth,

You will just scream 'Holy Jesus Fuck.'

That is when she will dance for you

Tell you its all over and you did so well,

tasted so good, self destructed like Art.

But your still not allowed to say her name.

Sister Machinegun

Such a silly girl
With her flowers and hollow-points
Your Tragedy such a lure-

Like confusion;
A fish drowning in the desert
Or a condom on a corpse

Your lies are as unimportant
As your truth no ones allowed to see.

Something too bad to be true
Is just as unbelievable
As 3am promises
Or paring knives that dice brick

No matter how you're sliced
There's still no way to prove you feel

And no matter what you say
I still don't believe you're real.

Hate Mail #8.

There's a lot of reasons you never

Ever, sleep with a writer.

Get it yet? We tell the world.

And there's no real stopping of

The Truth, or whatever I designate.

Someone, somewhere, somewhen,

Will believe it.

Its big T truth little girl.

Plato is all over it and you

Lovely, squirmed under it deliciously.

But to be honest you lied.

As much fun as it was,

To watch your disgust;

I forced your own fantasies on you.

I'm almost sick, almost.

And now you see; though

Why, why, why, you can NEVER just

Pretend for a chameleon and get by

Don the black and call yourself a freak

Because there's so much more you can't

Fucking handle that goes along with the title.

And I'll show you it all, dearest.

I'll ask for just one white paper kiss

And I'll leave scars---

See the light.

Morning can come as such a cruel haze
as unwelcome as ice water
down the back of your neck.

There is a man on the television who says;
you dont have to be like this
you can break free
I can cure you, fix you, make you whole.
Just buy my book.

I am no longer convinced it is that simple.
No one just wakes up and sees the light.

There is a philosophy of the crash.
I stumbled onto it, entirely by accident
the first time I woke up to find my revolver
with a pink sock pulled over the barrel.

Some people are just made to burn
in cheap hotels and shitty apartments

they creep and they wait, they smoke and they
fuck.

All with no sense of failure.

How do they do that?

That is a book I would buy at 3am.

I would drop $29.95 on that secret

that complacency with idling, with just
surfing

along and no longer giving a fuck

because surely, what you have is better than
nothing.

That light must sure be hypnotic.

Its a sedated American dream.

Do nothing, be nothing, be left alone.

Politics? Religion? Leave that shit to the
suits.

Have a piss poor beer and watch American idol

take your pill and the world will still be
there

in the morning.

Like the sock, the pistol and the red panties

pressed into your book like a flower,

All still there-

to be found years later.

Now you will never forget that girl

even if it took you years to realize it.

Life has a way of getting dark, flitting right
past

especially if you don't want to see that
light:

That saving grace, that hammer to break the
glass

around your heart and pull all the nails

from your brain.

There is nothing natural about the ache

there is nothing safe about the medicine

the light is not getting any closer

and goddamn the night is not getting any
shorter.

I think someday I will burn down my apartment.
Smash all the bottles and bury all the pipes
throw this chair right off the balcony
drive my car straight into the river,
just as fucking fast as it can go.
Wipe it all, start over. Go to the light.

      Maybe...

   but not today. Give me back my bottle
   come back to bed
   I will shut the blinds up tight

     That light is getting awfully
bright.

       And we don't need that
right now.

Blue.

Blue, you made self destruction so sexy

I wanted to lick your every scar,

Watch as you bled by the little roller, made
for plexi-

Glass; but used on flesh. An odd orgasm

Like your scream when I rolled the car.

Blue, you made self destruction so easy

An art, almost. Like expensive phone sex

That always ended with pain, in a deserted bar

Where you cried, and they asked you if you
liked older men.

Under My S(k)in.

Shoot me up again-

I never liked your fake red hair

any more than I

did tracing your track marks.

Your just a ghost, girl.

But we play rock star like no one else.

Barricade that door now-

come back to bed.

Do we really feel alive?

Here like this; cooperative suicide

might be the proper term.

I'm all out of ink

and I don't think you can spell sober.

That is really bad coming from me.

This here is a delicate thing-

This crucifixion of pills and liquor

like dancing with a train

-blindfolded

and maybe drunk.

Its all just a big bad idea

plain to see for anyone not involved

but its real- so real

And they will all ask for the details anyway

Vicarious, I suppose.

But its not meant for them to enjoy

Our twist of doom in a glass of gin

It comes down to this:

This anger, this nerve

this edge, this taste.

Rusted, twitchy-

You could be so very pretty

If you would just

shut the fuck up and give me back my goddamn
notebooks.

Hamlet had it right.

I think I have finally figured

out what I want in life:

Its not a car-

Its not a house-

Its certainly not a job-

It could be a time bomb,

maybe a shiny new pistol.

    No, no- stay with me here.

Listen. Hamlet knew.

Its that potential, that one second

that saves or damns, there is no second chance

    If you do it just right-

I love that simplicity.

I don't need a penny

    I don't need a pretty

I would carpet bomb my self first

Truly;

All I want is not to want.

Mary Mary Jane.

Bliss.

I have reached you,

if only for a moment.

Like warm bath water

numbing, enveloping.

I can drift, a moment

separated entirely

from myself

from my head

from the world.

   An existence

  both pure and meaningless.

     where you forget

     where you level

     where suddenly,

     deceptively

     nothing matters.

Its such a cute little lie

how it turns and flirts,

beckons from the distance in the middle of the
day.

   Calling you back:

     I'm right here. Just right here.

     All you have to do is find me.

          then its not so bad

          then it doesn't slip away as
fast

          then you are brain damaged and
happy

            just for a few moments

Relapse.

In the piercing glow of morning

that came too soon,
I groped in the darkness and found

a mass of hair and a wooden heart.

Beautiful and tragic

inspecting the blank of the wall for truths

that wont be found.

Write it off, unwarranted advice,

push it to the back of your head;

bury betrayal with pretty things,

blame me for knowing where to lay lips

for knowing what to whisper.

This is a pit with slick walls.

She crawled out once before;

but I stayed floating, right there.

To drag her back down,

another dose of poison with a smile

and even I, the Devil, know not why.

Red Panties-

How many days?

    How many days?

        How many dies?

    Wow. That wasn't even intentional.

    How many days have you died.

    How many days have you killed yourself?

        What the fuck are you trying to
prove?

    Who is even watching

        While you kill yourself these days?

It was cool a few years ago. You were crazy
but you were fun.

Then you took it too far, threw them all away

Because they couldn't keep up

    That was it

    Wasn't it?

    Yeah, yeah it was.

    Lies. Seriously. What the fuck?

    Come on, its cyclical, just
like you said.

    Throw them away, do the same
old shit

    Find new people to pretend:

    Its all a new issue

  Haha, funny?

    No maybe not.

    Alright, I'm sick.

    Problem, issues,

     Sure, fuck, whatever
you want to call it.

I want to tell you, so bad, shut up, fuck you!

The whole world is dying

Every heartbeat, every breath

It doesn't matter

Life is kind of like rape

you don't even have to ask for it

then your dancing in red panties

just so it doesn't ask for so much.

How fucked is that?

Seriously. What got into my head? What is my deal?

I don't know anymore. And I'm finding it harder and harder

to care.

'War'

Fuck this

There is no oppression

Only depression

There can be no change

There is no way out

No one cares

No one has

No one will

Addiction is purpose

Far more than subsistence

Death the terrible end

To something we take for granted

Anyway

I want to breathe smoke

This is my holy war

Against myself.

A follow up letter to the Dean
while eating runny eggs on a hangover.

Dearest Dean whoever,

        I hope you enjoyed the optomism and innocent candor
of my last letter. I really do need that academic suspension
lifted, after all.I used lots of positive words and went on
and on about being an adult, a new person, a changed man.

        Well. If you believed it perhaps I do have a future
in literature because it was all lies.

        If I have learned anything in these last few years
it is that I am really good at lying, fabricating, covering
my ass and just plain making shit up. I am an alcoholic
who wont say the word out loud, a silver tongued idiot who
buys into his own bullshit and a self destructive, over-
dramatic mess with serious doubts about his own mental
health.

        Maybe I belong in the university setting; that
crippled little world of psuedo-intellectuals who cant
exist elsewhere.Maybe we deserve eachother, is what I am
getting at.Misery loves company and all that shit.I am
certainly not coping in the ¦real world¦ with the job and
the mentally stunted adults who can somehow still look at
themselves every day after doing the EXACT same job, exact
same shit with the exact same people for thirty years.

        I cant do it. I cant handle that. I have said the
same five sentences to the same four people day after day
for the last month and a half. I would rather jump in front
of a train than keep doing that.

        So. The big point here. Let me come back to school.
Intelligence and complacent happiness dont go together at al
and I dont know what else to do anymore.

                                        Regretably yours,

                                        R. O'Hanlon

Deconstruction.

The first thing I took the razor to was my
tongue;

a squirming mass of flesh best at twisting-

words, truths- meanings and weightless
promises.

I shoved it still writhing into my pocket.

But I could not stop there.

Its not passion if you hold back.

Its not a goodbye kiss if you hold back.

I stabbed a screwdriver through my eardrums

both of them- there can be no talking me down

not this time, not this fucking time.

Pop, pop, silence;

        blood;

          conviction.

    I broke every mirror in the place with my
forehead.

    I felt warm and wet and alive.

    I swallowed, rather than spit.

I choked, rather than cry.

I took my left foot off at the ankle with an
ax.
There is something pathetic about walking tall
when your spine is turning to rust.
Oxidation. A fancy word for decay:

        Do it slow its rust-

        Do it fast its fire.

    I set the bed on fire.
I left my tongue there in a tangle of sheets.
To roast, to twitch, to decay.

        I limped away and hammered nails

        right up under my nails

If you have ever wanted to see God cringe
give that one a shot or five.

          One word and it could be over
but that's right, I took my ears

        and you don't have a weapon to raise

I broke your jaw, kicked in your teeth

      took a hammer to your knees, then
mine.

   Its only fair. After all.

   The smoke is making it hard to breathe,
but there is so much to be done.

   No, no- not done; undone.

Mud.

Some days I wish I were blind
Like blonde surfer boys in July.
Perception is lover to deception,
So I see the key as eliminating perception

By drink, by needle, by powder; buy roses
For the girl next door who hides her smile
And the little scars under her hair.
She'd be so happy if I hadn't noticed.

But I always notice the rust.
Even after we cut out my eyes
I can see you standing there
Disappointed because I had to ask.

I had to know, had to understand.
Why, I laugh quietly, inexplicably
When the cabbie asks if I'm headed home
But I only want to strangle the word from him.

Why I'm the child, crying with head in hands
But my hands hold the murderous potential

Of flame and 9mm lead. The potential to make
Understanding a mute point, if only

I could stop shaking, or dreaming.
Maybe that's the real ticket,
Explosive understanding of a dying
Brain, flying as all the blood seeps away.

Or maybe it's just another dead end.
Bullets are only as real as roses;
Really, and both can wound so deep
But it's worth a try, panicked eyes see so
much.

Even when you know your eyes don't see
Because life goes on even with the blindfold
And you can't prove anyone really exists,
Outside of how they affect you.
Wave goodbye to what you are
Your muse is a lying whore
And someday you will see nothing at all
And that's when it will all make sense.

Hate mail #13

I woke up today
tangled as ever, I swear
you fight me in your sleep
and always end up on top.

There was a stillness, a stale
the air isn't right;
like gun smoke, or the haze of large burn
I don't think the sun wanted to look
I should have noticed right away.

One of us was smoking in bed again
I'm wearing ashes like warpaint.
Better than blood, I would wager
Anyway, I took your vodka away
You were cradling it like a baby.

Its that first step off the bed
that really is telling, revealing
of just how hard you fell the night before.

Its not until I've thrown up and realized
that my toothbrush is nowhere to be found
that I notice you still haven't stirred
and you certainly aren't

Breathing.

Supernova

What do you want?

Not to want.

I thought it was simple.
I've said it before.
I want to live like a star-

Glow, glow, glow
darkness all around me: regardless.

Or something.

Maybe I want to be like a supernova.
I want to explode!

I want to exist so violent and clear
that no one
within a million light years
can deny

that I ever was.

...

But the darkness gets in.

It always does.

You can call self destruction art

but in the end your just talking to

and killing;

yourself.

Stars that fizzle don't even get names.

Nebula are only impressive because they must have been

something fucking great; only before

anyone was watching.

Unhealthy

This is no ordinary desert, my Darling.

Here we are forsaken faces in white heat.

A Skeleton faced Harlequin and I, her favorite,

The hot blooded Mescaline slave.

The sun refuses us heat, My Love.

For we are forgotten bits of pretty meat.

Leeches of the concrete catacombs,

And vampires to the bountiful wastes.

Your fangs are not in your mouth, Precious.

But somewhere desired and entrapping.

Hidden, alongside the heart you chewed,

From my chest; just to prove you could.

We are one, My Pretty Hate Machine.

Twins of dark mind, oddly colored souls.

Mutual abuse is our way to relate,

To the whispers in your skull, the devils in my flesh.

Our game is over now, My Dear.

This is our escape from where we never asked to go.

Your life drizzles into my hands like so much chocolate syrup,

And cold steel rests expectantly against my temple.

Surfer Rosa.

Rosa said she was a surfer.

I asked what the fuck, then, was she doing in Nebraska.

She said she lived there, like it should have been obvious. Rosa carried a switchblade and said her religion was rock and roll.

I was having a crisis. I couldn't seem to make sense of the world anymore. That is why I wound up there in the center of the country. In a state so flat even the people seem crushed and minimized.

I thought that maybe I was dying and this was some kind of pilgrimage; a death march of my own design. I had been drinking since noon and Rosa was very beautiful. She had way too much life in her for a place like this.

I felt like a vampire when I kissed her later that night. I felt like I was sucking at some of that long hair and vibrant soul she held. I was going to drink the surfer right out of her veins.

Or something.

I fucked Rosa in the tall grass outside
the bar around midnight. We were going to do
it in the car like teenagers but locked the
keys inside and she kept talking about stars.
It was good. Rosa kept telling me to cum but I
couldn't. There was something missing. Hearing
Rosa breathe and feeling her warm wet just
made me feel cold and dead again.

So I faked it and told Rosa she was
beautiful. She curled into my side and I lit a
match. Rosa said something in Spanish. I
didn't understand. I really didn't understand
any of it. I threw the match into the tall
grass around us. All it did was smoke a little
and die out.

Bony ass and white shoes.

You like tattoos
I like blondes

I couldn't have made you up if I tried
sitting there in the Key West mug
well into my sixth drink

Oh I like this, you touched my shoulder.
Your fucking adorable, I was already drunk.

You did shots like you honestly believed
catching up was safe.
It takes a certain type of person
to travel all alone, we agreed

Your shots had names:
    Alice in wonderland
    poets punch
    red headed slut
    liquid cocaine

You said your name wasn't important

and that you were a hooker

so I should stop looking at your skirt.

           Fine, okay, sorry.

           I mean, good. I don't want a

hooker.

           Another drink?

Oh Yes.

Introducing Mr. Self Destruct.

It turns out I don't miss you at all.
I miss your influence on me.
Your blood and your skin
and the way you made me breakfast
when I was fantastically hung over.

Its still those mornings
when I think I hear you there-
up cleaning because I broke something
or spilled something, or tripped on something

Or maybe just fucking smashed something.

I can be so very Hollywood.
And you told me once, amidst a breakdown
that that the only thing I wasn't passionate
for-
the only thing I was ever comfortable with-
was you.

    You said at least if I hit you,

you would still know I felt something.

I couldn't hit you
I wouldn't have stopped.

Not much of a poet these days, am I?
More of a ranty fuck with a drink in his hand.
Still talking about the girl from years ago
I kind of wish I could shut myself up
sometimes
but its not happening.

I am like a smack addict
your my heroin, baby.
I don't even have to see you and I am sick.
Sick like cancer
I cant even cut you out
not if I want to keep my brain, or hell
my useless fucking heart, in one piece.

So there you go. I am a cripple,
you were my legs, my spinal cord
and I traded you for...

Well this is the question. What do I have now?

What did you get replaced by?

I bet you are dying to know.

Fuck it. Whats left to lose?

This is so unhealthy.

How cool is a sea of meaningless pussy?

Awesome, right up until you start drowning.

Or wait, maybe that's the alcohol.

Either way; drowning.

I think I am in the final stage

when there is no air left and all your cells
are screaming

lungs burning, muscles spazzing

its as frantic as it is desperate.

Ill drag anyone down with me,

just for another half second of air.

Speaking of unhealthy...

Why do people glorify this shit?

This isn't even a poem.

Its a rant. What do you think is in my blood
tonight?

I meant to take just one

its how the game goes isn't it?

Chicken, by yourself.

Pill after pill. Maybe you get real serious,

lick the dust out of the bottle-

wash it all down with your end of the world
scotch.

You never really know

each binge could be THE ONE.

Couldn't it?

With no excuses left maybe its not even an
accident.

If its become a habit, can it ever be
unintentional?

Relax. If I was suicidal I would use my gun.

Nothing says fuck the world quite like

a .357 hollow point, tucked up under your chin.

Its this desperation that I blame on you.

I think you were my safety net.

Or better the safety on my trigger.

I have gone off spectacularly without you there to judge.

I am two people

the guy who just wants to write

and Mr. Self Destruct

who doesn't have fucking time to write anymore.

But he's got plenty of this.

Unfinished

So last night I stayed up
all night-
drinking coffee and frying bacon
strip by strip.

Until it was red and firm
pooling with grease and grit
basically wood and inedible.

And that made me think of you
      -and that made me add whiskey to my
coffee.

You are still like a red light
slipping through my blinds
and bringing some bit of the world into my
room.

Entirely Unwelcome, If I can be fucking
honest.

Ode to an Asshole

Hickory, Dickory, Dock!

You are a bitch that keeps looking at the clock,

When all I know and all I want

Is for you to suck some cock.

I told you I don't do romantic

Insisting is just pedantic

So twirl your hair and purse your lips

I'll sit here and pen an ode to your tits.

They are as round as the moon is chaste,

As Jon would say "I want them in my face".

Another drink, maybe two, ten or four!

When my words go over your head your panties hit the floor.

It has never taken too much before

Your brain is wired like a teen-lit whore.

So I'll toss in a three, a thou and a thus

To fill your eyes with a confused dumb lust.

And then we will go, we will go to bed

I'll get what I want and sleep like the dead;

And all the whole you are shouting and rocking the bed

I'll be composing you this in the back of my head.

Rambling about love

Part I

I told her then I didnt believe in t rue love
  and the way she exhaled you wuld think
i had hit her.

I still hear it now, like shebbreathed me out
  gave me up, ehh hunhh...

I meant it, but not in that final and chaste
HOLLYWOOD sense.
I think love is dirty, something that hurts and hits
and bites and shits and gets too drunk to walk.

Real love isnt true, real love makes men mad,
seduces them right out of their sanity
                right the fuck out.
Real love is worse forwomen,
                i imagine
makes them slaves, jealous. Angry.

        perhaps i have never met a woman
  who was truly in love.
      after all- i say i dont believe it
  and why would somehne who did have to prove it?

  that would be mad as religion.

The two biggest killers of men.
              love, true or not
                  and
              religion, true or not.

    ehh uhhhh...
            breathe.

Rambling about love   10/8/11

Part II

A wise man once compared love to vodka.

      -its wonderful, he said. Even if people can
actually smell it on you.
      -its great, he said. Right up until you have
had too much. then its time ti fight or puke on shoes.
      -its fantastic, he said. In that it makes you
stupidly happy. You grin like a fuck, maybe turn
backflips or decide not to flip cats in the same manner.

Well then this wise man started putting cigarettes out
on his great and exposed belly.

      why would you do that? I asked him.

      oh thats the other thing about love and vodka.
he told me. Then he held a butane tornh to his tongue
and never spoke again.

            Maybe he wasnt so wise.
            Maybe he was just drunk.
              -or in love.

Choke

Language closed like a vice,
A slow crushing of the throat
By a mind that understands,
But has no desire to share

Its secret, the reason why
It gets up every day.
Like an insect with 24 hours
To live, hate, love, and die.

Language closed like a tomb,
Around an understanding of playdough
Reality malleable to eyes that don't
See, but simply convey.

Then maybe it's just all figments,
Just the musing of a dying mind.

💣 Apology. 💣

I get three words today!
Go fuck yourself…
How'd you like to find that in your pants?
Is it wake up the chicks and break out the camera *awesome*?
Or is it just something we commemorate,
Maybe with a new tattoo, or a welding torch
Deep inside an amateur porn star's- uh eye?

If you can be nothing else you're at least dead
Right? What more can wolves teach other than
To bite, bite, bite until you've bled out or won.

The marshmallows make it fun, so sit the fuck back and open your
eyes I can't drive any faster. So ya fuck, how the fuck? What the
fuck? Fuck you, you fuckin' fuck who fucks fuckin' fucks.
Christmas is a time for sleazing; smashed windshields are just a sign
of affection. He says he'd draw a picture but his fingers won't stop
shaking. The cat is a lesbian but the lesbian is a man. If your thirteen
and curious he'll meet you on the corner.

Just tell yourself it's not real, it's not real. It's as real I want it
to be little momma.

And we're only safe here in the dirt. It doesn't matter that I'm
bleeding it should only scare you if it suddenly stops. Do you feel it
Alice? Is your brain vibrating through the mud yet? Please baby
please don't be dead.

But in the end it's all just energy. A synapse here or a
misfired synapse there. It's just chance to become priest, or maybe
predator. Evolution has always favored the predator. One little zap, a
fraction of a volt deep in grey Goo to decide if you're Charlie
Manson or just a confused hippie. The zap is the play, I say; and
wonder. How many zaps did it take to send this fake as shit 'holiday
tree' crashing through my front window, and the dog running with a
yelp. How many?

How many more until I'm Tommy Lee? Or buzzing through the bumbling bitch veins of Paris Hilton with nothing but camera flashes and lingerie?

Zip, zip, zap. You're an animal, you've just forgotten.

I have an easier time conversing with killers than classmates. Who does that make you?
1) Zip
2) Zap
3) ....

Three

I.

I can trace your every detail in my sleep.

From the dangerous guitar curve of your hips,

The cruel warmth of your lips

To drowning depths of siren blue eyes.

I've tried to murder your sweet memory.

From the haunting scent of your hair at 3am,

The taught tap of my fingers on your navel,

To figments of your breathing just out of reach.

II.

I already envy whoever you'll love next.

I want your voice after midnight ringing,

I crave your flirting fingers after nights alone,

My arms are lead, without you in them.

I'll never again say three little words,

Without tripping over pieces of you.

Whoever hears them next wont see,

Wont know I'll never fully mean it.

III.

Or maybe you're here, and I've gone blind.

Your pale skin has become glass,

Your voice a steamy nothing in my ears.

The words I clung to a bruise,

Self inflicted affection,

And I just made you up to hurt myself.

With Her

It's a street where locked doors encourage
theft,

And I'm advised to stay close.

It's a house where boots rest near cheetah
print converse,

And the table serves chicken and cocaine.

It's a place where neon eyes heal with smoke,

And conversations have no bones.

It's a cluttered room where we share her
friend's bed,

And violent music beats against the chipping
walls.

It's a small corner of the bed that smells of
young flesh,

Smoldering cigarettes and old flannel.

It's a gentle, innocent touch,

In a world of concrete chaos.

It's kind, dark eyes that haunt and linger,

bringing dreams as soon as I've left her side.

Rabbit Hole--

So I slipped and I fell
and things just got steeper
I tumbled and rolled
and just dropped even deeper.

Alice got lucky
She never fell this far.
Way down here are doors best locked
-not ajar.

Too late for that now
fates come to collect.
Just what are you,
when you are what your mind must reject?

How sloppy my rhyme
how arrogant my time.
is that a light I see,
beginning to shine?

Or just my reflection,
some oil on the rocks.
Perhaps this is hell
I always pictured more clocks.

Maybe melted and strewn,
All over the place,
like Dali on a rampage
with acid, cocaine, strippers and lace.

Things just got weird, yeah?
but not weird enough (never).
Where we are headed-

this is nothing, normal, a good day,
Fucking kids stuff.

So the bottom was false
I burst right on through
and suddenly I didn't mind
because I was no longer like you.

I'll be falling forever
I cant be bothered to scream.
Ill keep on counting the layers
in this red and beautiful dream.

Going mad isn't so hard
you just have to jump.
Don't falter now and don't you dare try to
cling
All you will do then is ruin this thing-

For the rest of us
who are no longer afraid.
Sober and crazy-
if I could bottle it I'd get paid.

But I cant and I wont
so go try but don't-
for there's no way to tell
if we will share this hell
and your fall must be your own
because for all I know, I have actually flown.

End.

About the Author.

    Robert O'Hanlon Jr. is a recovering poet and aspiring writer from Manchester NH where he lives with his muse and their miniature schnauzer. Robert is a student of English at Manchester Community College and a ten year veteran with a local hospital.

    Robert wrote the preceding poems five to seven years ago and likes to think he has grown up a bit. Or at least the whiskey has gotten more expensive.

Made in the USA
Middletown, DE
27 September 2017